SEASONAL R
2007 S

CW01582374

WINTER SOLSTICE

Giving to Yourself

No. 12 (December)

The Collected Works of Gregge Tiffen

P SYSTEMS PUBLICATIONS
LA JOLLA, CA

All material for The Collected Works of Gregge Tiffen
is edited and published by P Systems
First Edition 2007
Second Edition, 2016
Published in the United States of America

P Systems
P.O. Box 12754
La Jolla, CA 92039
858.658.0665
www.p-systemsinc.com/publications

These booklets are offered in appreciation for the ancient mystical teachers and their messenger, Gregge Tiffen.

The Collected Works of Gregge Tiffen

The Story of Infinity (2011)

First Encounter - The Trilogy (2010)

Vol 1: Into the Universe: Extraterrestrial
Vol 2: Down to Earth: Terrestrial Activities
Vol 3: Earth and Second Earth

Life in the World Hereafter: The Journey Continues **(2006)**

Booklet of the Month Series:

Gregge's desire was to have booklets sized to easily fit into your shirt pocket or time manager. You can open to any page wherever you are and receive concise and inspiring messages from Gregge's original works. Each series has twelve booklets organized by months of the year.

Now available or coming soon online:

2016-Echoing Series (Booklets 2, 3, 4)
2012-Echo (Booklet 1)
2011- Open Secrets Series (Booklets 1-12)
2010- The Journey Continues Series (1-12)
2009- Language of a Mystic Series (1-12)
2008- Lessons in Living Series (1-12)
2007- Seasonal Reflections Series (1-12)
2006- Winter Solstice: The Christmas Story
INDEX Booklets of the Month (2006-2012

Contents

Part I

The Planet's Birthday[1]

I will give you everything I am because I am not prepared to keep it. I am self-contained therefore never diminished by giving.

Every mystical school considers winter solstice as the apex of the year. In ancient times this particular cycle was the most important celebration of the year. It marks the beginning of a new yearly cycle for the earth, and it has always been treated with the greatest respect identifying the birth with joy and celebration.

The whole atmosphere and meaning of the season is significant and, as the planet's birthday, we are all in attendance.

We are the celebration.

---

[1] The marvelous Christmas Story told by Gregge Tiffen is also available as an e-booklet on Amazon entitled ***Winter Solstice: The Christmas Story.***

Much of the tradition that we see today comes from eons of time ago when similar celebrations of singing and dancing occurred then as it is meant to be now with gift giving as our means of expression.

It seems each year that more and more people are asking themselves what this season should *really* mean. What is it designed to be and can it be celebrated differently? It is unfortunate that this event of renewal has come to be celebrated in such mundane forms because nothing is more significant in our own on-going growth and development than this particular season; there is a reason for such importance.

Recorded history at best covers only about ten thousand years. However, the planet has been here eight and one-half billion years. The story we are considering here is as old as the planet itself, and it is a story that has always been here like it or not. And, it has always been updated with every new Messiah and with every new teacher who has contributed to its perpetuation.

In our current awareness, we have lost the story of the planet. That is what happens in the natural cycle of humanity just as when we were children we saw as children. Now as adults we are allowed to expand into a whole new arena of understanding.

What must occur is renewal.

There must be a perpetuation of *The Story* and in time the concept of Christmas as we now know it will no longer be. It will fade but the essence will not die because a new story will take its place. It will be of different attitudes, different concepts, and different awareness. Nevertheless, the foundation of the new story will still be very much as we have now.

With this in mind, let us consider the marvelous story that is biblical in the way we see it now, but it is not a story exclusive to Christmas. It can be found in The Bible: St. Luke, Chapter 2.

The story for the planet transcends any religious concepts and ideology; that means it is as valid for the Jews as it is for the Muslims, Hindus, Buddhists, and Christians. It is unfortunate that it has been identified as a Christian story because that defines it in a category applicable to a certain group of people as if, "this is mine and it is not yours." *Nothing* could be further from the truth.

What we have is an updated continuation of a very old story; a story of the planet as told through a human event. In this event the story begins with a mother and father, Mary and Joseph - a story about birth but not the birth of a baby. It is the story of a conception that can only come from a higher power. A source from heaven or spiritual, if you like; metaphysical, if you like; or mystical, if you like. Nevertheless, it transcends any concept of originating in the mundane.

It would not have been unusual if Mary's husband, Joseph, had impregnated her. We certainly would not look upon that as unusual. Women become pregnant by their husbands all the time. That tells us that the story is symbolic. The only way it can be told is symbolically in order that it can be carried forth into infinity.

As a virgin Mary represents a source that is untouched and untainted, in any manner, by the mundane. She represents a whole new belief far beyond normalcy that cannot be attached to tradition taking the story completely beyond human limitations.

For instance:

- How many virgin birth do you have in any given year?
- How would it have been accepted at that time if they had had the communication abilities we have today?
- What if word had gone out that there was a woman who was pregnant through a direct act from heaven?

You now have some idea of what kind of havoc that would have caused!

It was not told that way in those times either because there was no need to tell it in commonplace language. It is representative of all things changing when you are receptive to the power of higher consciousness.

The gift you give to yourself is to be open and to make space for acceptance.

When we are receptive, we do not need any human element to tell us we are capable of receiving this marvelous gift, this marvelous conception. There is something that lies within us that we bring into this world, and this *something* transcends the body. It is divine in consciousness.

The babe is conceived in heavenly consciousness as applied to the human level just as there is a part within each of us, male and female, that is a receptive womb; receptive to something that is divine and not a part of the world as we know it.

This is the story of the universe itself, of heaven manifesting directly to the human level saying, "Here in the purity we are planting this seed. Here is where a birth is untouched and unaffected by human elements. Here is the purity of beginning."

What a magnificent promise that in any instant, at any time, and in any atmosphere we are always *potentially* prepared to be impregnated with the divine seed.

This is the story of life. This is not the story of a season. It is a message that says: That which happens here, happens always and to everyone. It is a promise that can be received and manifested at any time and under any circumstance.

The child itself is the gestation of your own idea, your own awakening, and your own awareness deep within you.

What you know is what you know about yourself.

What heaven gives you is not some off-handed unimportant message. What heaven gives you is the reality of your power to impregnate your life.

Remember that the whole story deals with a new beginning. That indicates a cycle that is finished *is* finished. What is done *is* done. You cannot go back and change one element of it.

An extremely important message of the story is to complete the pregnancy and to move into a new phase of life in order to give to maturity that which you have nurtured. The year finishes. The cycle completes itself and at that point a new birth is inevitable. A new idea is ready. In essence, a new you *is* ready to be born.

The greatest gift you give yourself is the departure from who you were.

- Give up the last year.
- Get rid of all those things of the mundane world.
- Make room for an awareness of a whole new spiritual understanding that will carry you throughout the next year's cycle.

This season is about giving up what you have and accepting a new awareness that now exists within you. It's the newness that is the meaningful part of the story. You are not required to hold on to an old part of what you were since the single greatest gift you give to yourself is to leave the old for the new you.

It is not the exchange of gifts with other people or the acceptance of gifts with other people that is the issue. It is the willingness to recognize that this is a new you prepared and ready to manifest. Your receptivity to what heaven has for you and will give to you is the story of what you will become. It is what you will give to the world in the coming year.

This new you is birthed in stillness and quietude. Enter the stillness that is a cleansing experience.

Silent Night

The first stillness is done honestly and simply in harmony with nature. You are alone with you. You commit to the harmony of earth and therein is stillness and quiet, peace and understanding.

Recognition comes when you leave the old and become the new. Heaven then recognizes what you have done and will act on your behalf in the coming year with all the necessary elements having been made to make sure you are recognized. When you become the new you, there is no mistaking that everything you need has been placed before you and *nothing* is going to change that.

You have given up the old you with tremendous love, not regret. After all you made it. It has not been easy and you probably did very well under the circumstances.

This letting go is, more than anything, a completion.

It is an attitude of, "I let go of myself first. I let go of my attitudes that I have assessed as good and bad. I let go of my wants and desires and of my fears and hopes. I let go of *everything.*"

You are going to say good-bye to some things you wish you did not have to say good-bye to in human terms, but you *are* going to say good-bye to them. You are then open, aware, and capable of accepting the new you, the new promise, the new gifts.

This new you, the person of quality, does not have to seek approval or to make overtures. The universal energy makes sure that those who need to find you seek you. Those people whom you need to make your life fulfilling seek your newness out. What more could you possibly need?

Your gift is to celebrate your own birth in your simplicity and in your purity.

This is a story that has been with us from the beginning of the planet, and it is a continuum of a reality on the planet. This is a story of heaven making a gift to you. This is your story of renewal to be realized by you. It always has been your story, and it was never designed or intended to be anyone else's story. And, the most interesting and lovable part is that it occurs every year.

This time belongs to each of you in a very significant way both individually and collectively.

A new promise.
A new gift.

It makes no difference two thousand or twenty thousand years from now. The story is still going to exist. The meaning of the story will not change.

What I would exhort you to, what I would give as a gift to you, what I would lay down a soul for, would be for your awareness to recognize that this is a personal event for your life. It is the time that has been set up on this planet for you and for heaven to be with each other without interference.

May the reindeers pull your sleigh across the rooftops and into the fertile green valleys of a truly new season with new awareness.

Part II
The Ten Gifts in the Temple of Ten

These ten gifts indicate the challenges offered as an acceptance of an interchange of knowledge where the essence of life is celebrated purged of the malfunctions of body, mind, and spirit.

The challenge of One:
This is the challenge for the first census to be taken within each of us to stand and be counted as a savior in our own lives as one-of - One.

The challenge of Two:
This is the challenge within each of us as a center point. It is the basis of all strength and the discovery of equality in balance.

The challenge of Three:
This is challenge within each of us to come to the awareness that now *is* the appointed time.

The challenge of Four:

This is the challenge within each of us to see the world as opportunity. Here is the arena for play, for work, for love, and for the full expression of self.

The challenge of Five:
This is the challenge within each of us to expand into change as change happens This is the discovery that which is greater than we ever expected.

The challenge of Six:
This is the challenge within each of us to gain a higher etheric appreciation of ourselves as we go inward in order to go outward into manifestation. Here is an expression of love's universal connection.

The challenge of Seven:
The challenge is within each of us to recognize that the more we know the more we need to know. We recognize this challenge as
upward bound buoyancy.

The challenge of Eight:
This is the challenge within each of us to admit to the responsibility of discharging

all opportunities for our own benefit. We accept personal responsibility for aging, for the use of money and for co-creation as examples of opportunities.

The challenge of Nine:
This is the challenge within each of us to acknowledge that we actually come closer to the infinite than we ever thought possible. It is here that we affirm our singular and unique reality on a universal level.

The challenge of Ten:
This is the challenge within each of us to renew awareness that everything that is mystically and spiritually true *is* true. We accept the full cycle in the world's pathway to accomplishment as the universe fulfills itself according to the Divine Plan.

Gregge Tiffen 1976

Information on other SEASONAL REFLECTIONS: Separate Kindle E-booklets on Amazon

January: The Significance of Beginning

This booklet reminds us of progress based on the significance we assign to our daily activities in terms of the personal power we recognize and accept. To believe otherwise is to continue life's journey as if we are blind while seeking our way out of the forest.

February: The Numerology of Love

Love, the most mysterious and powerful force on earth cannot be found. It is inherent in us from birth, but we hide our love from ourselves and from the world. Find out why, why and why?

March: It's Springtime: Flow with the Power of Nature

If life seems to be failing us, let's shake out our metaphysical carpets, throw off the heavy winter blankets and take a new stance, walk a new path, find a new answer, develop a new character, build a new body, and feel confident once again that a positive pathway is in front of us. Read on.

April: Tax Time: Are You Taxing Yourself?

Metaphysics, like life, is not a free ride. We are going to get out of it just what we put into it; no more and no less. It's not the winds of fortune or the vagaries of fate but more like learning how to ride a bike. Hang on, and let's get into the learning experiences as a top priority even at tax time. Discover the unlimited opportunities that are never dictatorial.

May: Mother Nature

Are we trusting, curious, enthusiastic adults, or are we part of a popular attitude of, "why bother? That bothersome sense of being diminishes golden opportunities to be willing adults. Discover our birthrights produced by our Mother - Nature - for us her children.

June: Father Time

Men are fascinated by time. They produce order by establishing a task within a time frame as an attempt to control. Male or female, let's listen when we tell ourselves that we don't have enough time. Is time flooding your mind and ruling your creative world? Discover how to reduce your dependency on time and become more harmonious with the planet and with universal cycles.

July: Feeding Freedom: The Meaning of Independence Day

Independence is most often thought of as selfish, isolated, and insensitive to others. The consideration here is that independence is our basic right to think, to develop in advance of others, to make decisions, and to fulfill that pattern that is distinctly yours. Discover your rights and determine how you are going to move through your daily experiences.

August: Do the Angels Take a Vacation?

Everything in life is a representative of the unseen in the process of manifestation on this planet with an infinite number of variables and conditions. Consequently this planet is set up to have incarnate and discarnate -

visible and a non-visible elements, but to reach out to an angel in supplication for deal making of some kind defeats the means and methodology of what Earth School is all about. Discover how the school system is designed in order for us to understand the reflective state of affairs.

September: What You Should Get from Education

Education under the best of terms is a precious commodity of life to renew, to challenge, to promise and to progress. *How* we use our experiences has a profound effect on how to help our spirits to find their places among the halls of spiritual reality. Discover the importance of your individuality in the whole scheme of life.

October: The Great Pumpkin: Was Charlie Brown Right?

Charlie Brown brought us a group of children and a dog posing adult questions and behaving as if they were bound to win while making choices that indicted they were determined to lose. In reality, a true cosmic joke! Maybe you can discover how to communicate by using the "poor little me," syndrome to at least make money in the world of entertainment. Otherwise, re-discover your self-identity song that is always sending out your message.

November: The Power of Giving Thanks

Discover the power of giving thanks and to be aware of what it is that we are receiving *within* our own experiences, *through* our own experiences, and *from* our own experiences inclusive of how where to begin, how to validate the information, and how to share with others. In the mystical schools, this point of contemplation is well understood on the basis for spirit to grow; there must be a point of identification.

December: the Winter Solstice: Giving to Yourself

The whole atmosphere and meaning of the season is significant as the planet's birthday, and we are all in attendance. We are the celebration! Are you among the people who are asking what this season should really mean and what it is designed to be? Discover the reason for its importance as a new beginning and a birth of personal significance.

About the Author

Gregge Tiffen received intensive training in mysticism and mystical law in the Far East. He returned to the United States in the late 1950's to teach as he was taught. Before his death in 2008, he was a well-respected business consultant, exceptional teacher, and personal counselor to people throughout the world. You can learn more about him and his work in his highly acclaimed book Life in the World Hereafter: The Journey Continues.

For a list of other publications, visit:
www.p-systemsinc.com/publications

P Systems
P.O. Box 12754
La Jolla, CA 92039
(858) 658-0665
mpatrece@p-systemsinc.com

12347829R00018

Printed in Great Britain
by Amazon